Machines to the Rescue

Fire Trucks

by Bizzy Harris

Bullfrog
Books

Ideas for Parents and Teachers

Bullfrog Books let children practice reading informational text at the earliest reading levels. Repetition, familiar words, and photo labels support early readers.

Before Reading

- Discuss the cover photo. What does it tell them?

- Look at the picture glossary together. Read and discuss the words.

Read the Book

- "Walk" through the book and look at the photos. Let the child ask questions. Point out the photo labels.

- Read the book to the child, or have him or her read independently.

After Reading

- Prompt the child to think more. Ask: Have you ever seen a fire truck? Would you like to?

Bullfrog Books are published by Jump!
5357 Penn Avenue South
Minneapolis, MN 55419
www.jumplibrary.com

Library of Congress Cataloging-in-Publication Data

Names: Harris, Bizzy, author.
Title: Fire trucks / by Bizzy Harris.
Description: Minneapolis, MN: Jump!, Inc., [2022]
Series: Machines to the rescue | Includes index.
Audience: Ages 5–8 | Audience: Grades K–1
Identifiers: LCCN 2020041854 (print)
LCCN 2020041855 (ebook)
ISBN 9781645279075 (hardcover)
ISBN 9781645279082 (paperback)
ISBN 9781645279099 (ebook)
Subjects: LCSH: Fire engines—Juvenile literature.
Classification: LCC TH9372 .H358 2022 (print)
LCC TH9372 (ebook) | DDC 628.9/259—dc23
LC record available at https://lccn.loc.gov/2020041854
LC ebook record available at https://lccn.loc.gov/2020041855

Editor: Jenna Gleisner
Designer: Molly Ballanger

Photo Credits: ryasick/iStock, cover; Tctomm/Dreamstime, 1; TennesseePhotographer/iStock, 3; theoldman/Shutterstock, 4; yanggiri/iStock, 5, 23tl; Maskot/Getty, 6–7, 23br; Manuel Esteban/Shutterstock, 8–9; JustPixs/Shutterstock, 10–11; Christine Bird/Shutterstock, 12–13; Oliver Perez/Dreamstime, 14, 23tm; djphotography/iStock, 15; davelogan/iStock, 16–17, 23tr; Keith Muratori/Shutterstock, 18, 23bm; 400tmax/iStock, 19; Wangkun Jia/Shutterstock, 20–21, 23bl; Shutterstock, 22; Flashon Studio/Shutterstock, 24.

Printed in the United States of America at Corporate Graphics in North Mankato, Minnesota.

This book is dedicated to Dave Meyers and his family. Thank you for your many years of dedication to the Columbia Heights Fire Department.

Table of Contents

Ladder and Hose

Lights flash at the fire station.

FIRE ALARM

alarm

The alarm rings.
Why?
There is a fire!

uniform

The firefighters get ready!
They put on uniforms.

They get in fire trucks.
They leave in a hurry!

fire
engine

fire
truck

light

Lights flash.

Sirens sound.

They let people
know to stay away.

They get to the fire.

The truck holds
the tools they need.

The fire engine carries water.

fire
engine

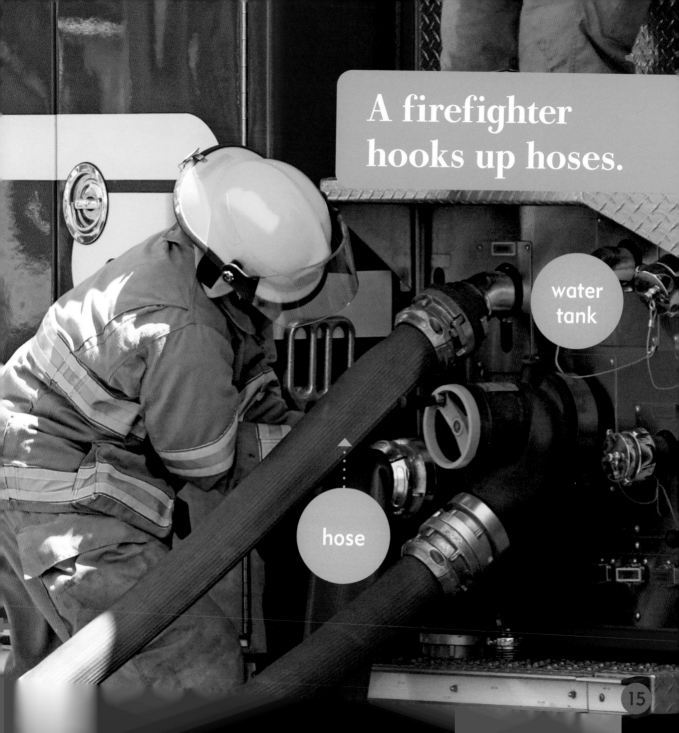

A firefighter hooks up hoses.

water tank

hose

The water helps
fight the fire.

The fire truck
has a ladder.

It is tall.

ladder

People climb down.
Everyone is safe.

19

The fire trucks go back to the station.

fire
station

FIRE RESCUE

FIRE/RESCUE
A2

LADDER 1

21

Fire Truck Tools

Take a look at some of the tools inside a fire truck!

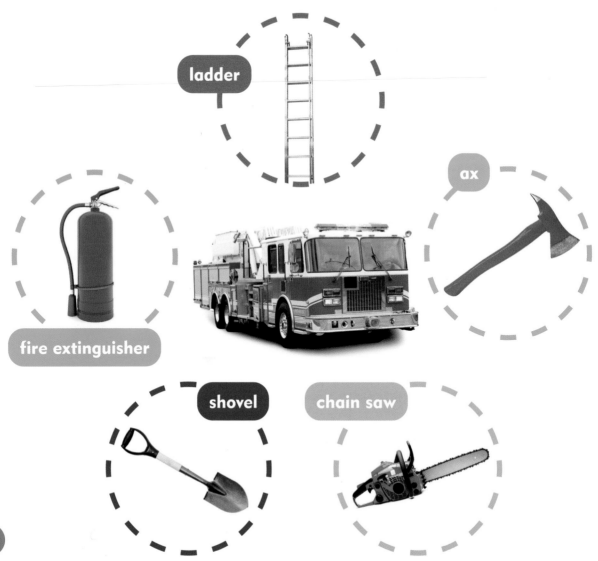

ladder

ax

fire extinguisher

shovel

chain saw

Picture Glossary

alarm
A device with a bell, siren, or buzzer that warns of danger.

fire engine
A truck that carries water and hoses for fighting fires.

firefighters
People who are trained to put out fires.

fire station
A building where fire trucks and engines are kept.

ladder
A structure that is used by people to climb up and down.

uniforms
Special sets of clothes worn by members of a group or organization.

Index

To Learn More

Finding more information is as easy as 1, 2, 3.

❶ Go to www.factsurfer.com

❷ Enter "firetrucks" into the search box.

❸ Choose your book to see a list of websites.